AF609866

Magnetized By Black Irises

Love and Other Emotions

by
Denise Kolanovic

Magnetized
By
Black Irises

Love and Other Emotions

Copyright © 2020 by Denise Kolanovic

Cover art:
Abstract Eye
Vincent Pierre

Words With Wings Press 2020

ISBN:
978-1-716-45540-7

All rights reserved. No part of this book may be reproduced or transmitted in any form or by any means without written permission of the author.

Dedication

I dedicate this book to my most cherished loves: my husband, Tonci; my daughters, Dana and Adrienne; and to my parents who taught me the meaning of love.

Special Thanks to Peter V. Dugan, J R Turek and Dr. Katherine Hogan for editing and incredible suggestions!

Preface

These poems are reflections of many emotions, especially love. They reflect self-love; love of life, nature and art, spiritual love, lack of love, lost love, platonic love, and love-hate relationships. They are a culmination of many years of self-realizations.

Table of Contents

The Man with White Stubble

The man with white stubble

Wears army fatigues from Vietnam.

They smell of urine.

His fingers are long and slim but rounded

At the tips, as if they'd been squeezed in a press.

He has dark, lifeless eyes

And a slow, slightly slurring voice

That is somehow very soft and sweet.

He is intelligent

But he has been dealt a bad hand.

The aliens don't like him.

He's African American.

He's literate but he's not normal

Anymore. He doesn't smile.

It doesn't matter if he is kind.

He has no address;

He can't receive mail.

He creeps in wherever there is warmth

And he makes no excuses;

He lives in the moment,

For there’s nothing there to lose.

Me and You

It seems I can't be rid of you.
Those days we were inseparable;
The nights were long, insatiable.
I thought that I was over you.
I see your face in front of me.
Your eyes are gazing steadily
Upon my lips, approaching me
On tip toe now, you're nearing me.
I sometimes miss your loving me
With strong, sure hands exploring me,
Your soft, warm lips remolding me
To part of you, you're part of me.
And though you're gone, I think of you
With anger past, rechargeable
With music now, comparable
To favorite songs; I dream of you.
In night landscapes I feel that you
Come fumbling to get next to me.

You sleep yourself inside of me

As if time's not kept me from you.

Your thought invades my secret mind

Exploding facts with fictional kind

That fit so well, like perfect rhyme

Intense, but not in real-life time.

So now I gather thoughts of you--

Like flowers they're perishable--

And place them so they're traceable

Till next I dare to dream of you.

Inarticulate

The name of the tongue knows the name of the heart
And the same goes around and around to the know.
In the pocket of speech lies the seed of the dream.
And the same goes around and around to the know.

The voice of the mind speaks the words of the soul.
And the same goes around and around to the know.
This is the way in and the way out.
This is the sense free from all doubt.
This is the know of eternity,
Of birds' wings and sunflower songs.
The know that is the breath and sparrows' music, the depth
Of rain-ice on evergreen tips which sway all winter long.

The voice of the mind knows the eyes of the heart.
And the same goes around and around to the know.

In the image of thought brings the meaning of life.

And the same goes around and around to the know.

With the sound of the wind do the echoes rescind

In the mountains and mix the oceans' motions.

The Second Chakra

Your back is in Downward Dog and your head
Nearly touches the ground.
Your kundalini spine is happy.
And in the uncertainty of "know" "not know," she returns.
Your lips quiver and you remember
How important your tongue is to her.
So you let it float to the roof of your mouth:
A sacred place where thoughts wait to be said.
You learn to examine your desires.
Divine Mother Sakti brings you honey.
You sit in the Lotus, your knees being
Pulled down perpendicular to the ground.
Your kundalini spine is straighter
And you are smiling.
You are lifted a bit higher as your neck
Stretches away from your shoulders.
You breathe and with each breath,

Your heart opens more and more until

You are the breath and there is nothing more

But glowing peace and radiance.

Massapequa Park Preserve

The robin redbreast has come home again
And pine cones fall as branches start to bud.
Spring skies hold heavy clouds that soon will rain
Upon the earth in slanted style, then mud
Will form from saturated earth until
The winds pick up and call the water back
To April skies. The newest blossoms still
Are not yet seen along the branches, black
And gray with specks of green. And soon the dust
will fall from trees to signal buds to burst,
that first chartreuse that looks like snow, but must
disperse in three days as Massapequa's first
attempt to clean the ground and then prepare
to green the earth and sweeten up the air.

First Love

I gazed at you through silver haze

Magnetized by black irises.

In thoughtless wonder I seemed soothed,

Drenched in bubbles of soapy security,

Until soaked and wrinkled, I gazed…

Dumbfounded.

I gazed, naked, in a steamy tub,

Bathing in shallow water.

At The Montauk Club

Purple flowers on a dais
Overlook the guests as lighted candles
Begin the celebration.
Lavender and hyacinth adorn
The tables in crystal vases.
We smell the sweet scents
And reflect on words conceived
In divine intangibilities.
Oh, lighted ceremony, entangle me
In your special power of tradition.
Let's listen to fiery truth songs
Chant the poetry
Arising from midnight contemplation.
Spring begins anew and sparkling suns filter through
Asphalt road blessed by our feet.

After Maxfield Parrish's *Daybreak*

She came to me at dawn.

Was it a dream?

Lurching over me, curiously crouching,

Searching my smiling face.

I opened my eyes and knew her embrace,

Though she had not touched me.

"Oh, angel," I called. I thought I called.

My voiced echoed between the two

Thick marble columns. She smiled back,

As the trees and mountains surrounded my body.

The twinkling of sunlight,

Pink and white dots, filled my vision.

"Oh, angel, touch me, save me," I cried again.

My voice was a million vibrations

Of tears and laughter, as she caressed my face

With fingertips and, in a flash, disappeared into daybreak.

I am a Fish

I am a fish swimming sideways,

Two gills breathing hydrogen and oxygen.

I am slivered by symmetry and silvered by iridescent scales

Pearlizing my center, related to my core, prismic,

If the sun can get down into my medium, my aqua-air,

My density of molecules.

You may not come into my domain of eel-song strategies

And replicated eternity. Here, it is silent and the two halves

Of myself are finally fitted.

Swimming is the perfect movement. It defies gravity

But it is not free of mass. There are caves and quagmires.

Water is pure but I am not:

I fall into the murkiness within each fathom.

I swim past coral and kelp, so deeply.

My halves are less important where I am.

I no longer fret over bigger fish and that means

Unblinking eyes and cold blood.

That means freedom from fear and doubt.

That means no emotions nor questions.

The Hunchback of Massapequa

Have you seen him, the hunchback?

He pushes his wagon

Along the sunrise highway

Day after day, shopping the curbs

For plastic bottles and cans.

His body is dwarfed by the highway

But you can glimpse his hunchback

If you check Fit Club's curb.

His wagon has just been emptied of cans,

As he chats to the woman next to the wagon.

A large suitcase in his wagon

Will be set aside for more cans

And plastic bottles, but for now, the hunchback

And his friend share coffee at the curb

Near businesses of the sunrise highway.

They're both tanned; she doesn't pick cans.

That's his job, to scan the highway.

Their transportation is bike or wagon.

Their domain is the summer's curb.

And she's protected by the hunchback.

I've wondered how many cans

He's gathered. Where does the hunchback

And his girl go with their wagon?

Has he enough coins to curb

Their hunger after the sun rises on the highway?

Even in my town, there's a hunchback

Who scans the asphalt curbs

To acquire coins from bottles and cans.

"The Unexamined Life Is Not Worth Living"
Acrostic Poem

That is the truth;

Having lived many years and

Examining each one but

Understanding

Not all that much, I pretend to know it all.

Every year begins a closer

X-ray of the details of my deeds,

After or before the deeds

Manage to have become realized.

Inasmuch as

No one really cares about my daily activities,

Eventually, I have learned to

Devour my time in order to experience

Love, joy, peace, pain, suffering and beauty

In all the paths on which I walk.

For all things are important,

Especially the little things that are swept

Into a closet

So that no one knows their secret importance.
Now, as I get closer to comprehending why
Old age is a time for reflection,
Terrific cognizance shows me the big picture
Where I see patterns forming.
Otherwise, I would just go along my merry way,
Regardless of my decisions,
Thereby creating this journey and
Heirs of my
Legacy.
In all things,
Vivid memories do not haunt me.
Insight replaces hindsight
Now and hopefully, in the future.
God willing.

North Wind

It is dark upon the mountain
And the snow is coming hard
And the moon is barely shining
On the trees beyond the yard.
And the lone apparent movement
Is the wind upon the trees
It is vicious in its pushing
So randomly the leaves.
But this is winter’s duty
And we can only watch
Its annual performance
Till the very end of March.
But there’s beauty in the breathing
Of the air upon the earth,
Otherwise invisible;
We’d hardly know its worth.

Though the howling and screeching

Can cause us some concern,

It's surely quite exciting

To see the snowflakes turn.

Ma Sympatique

Sister, where are you my lovely girl,

My lovely girl.

Sister, where are you my sweet *jeune fille?*

Where have you gone, all alone, all alone

In the waves of the ocean, the navy blue sea?

What do you see there? Are you all alone,

Are you alone and where is he?

You danced very little and played very fast.

You kissed us with abundance and played very fast.

You swayed to the music and hit from the middle.

You pushed up away and up to the riddle.

You gathered us in your arms

And sang songs.

Sister, where are you my lovely girl,

My lovely girl?

Sister, where are you my sweet *jeune fille*?

Have you flown from the water,

Gushed and sprayed the shorelines

Toward your Paris?

Are you now happy and whole

And kissing your soul and where is he?

Where is he, your darling, your sweet lover?

Is he with you, my darling, my sister,

My closest rainbow of life,

My pretty baby sister, my sweet little girl?

For Flora and Giovanni: Leaving the Nursing Home

The front door brought in the frozen wind.

She threw herself on the bed fumbling to find warmth.

Her teeth were gone.

“Flora, what are you doing here?”

“Where are your shoes?” Giovanni asked

“I left them at the home. I didn’t think I’d need them again.

But look at me, I can walk!” Flora beamed.

She smiled showing a gaping mouth and protruding chin.

“You’ve become quite thin,” he smiled.

“Yes, I’m thinner than I ever was, John,

so you can’t call me “fatso” anymore,” she laughed.

“And what are you doing here?” You’ve been gone

over twenty years. You left me alone, but I see you again,

as if time has not changed.”

She reached out a wrinkled hand to touch him.

“No, don’t touch me. I’m like the clouds, like the smoke

Of my tiparillos." Giovanni haunted.

They both laughed.

He sang to her in Italian, she sobbed,

For they were both free.

When the Squire Comes

For Adrienne and John

You steal them from us.

You, the abysmal squire who takes away

our kings and queens,

tearing our hearts with your fangs and poison daggers

ripping into softness, once protected

by perfect unicorn dreams.

You are the second guesser of strange

circumstances that strip

our inner voice, a flame,

so that dull droning sounds escape

and we, entrapped in fearful contemplation

and isolated rage scratch our skin against cement.

We scream the dreadful cries of Antigone,

who drags again her brother's bloody body from the vultures.

We taste the sour metal flavor of blood

for we have gnawed our tongues in curses to you.

You wretched power,

Go to your world of currents, of whirlpools

that roam the earth. Go!

You open shadow doors to our blurred vision
and we must gain composure from your fission
of madness and disparity.
When wondering reddens all thought
and unwelcome devils gloat
in our despair, we sit silently
waiting for the semblance of pure snow.
And in the whitening moment of eye blink
the colors become clearer and the center stage
is set again of new vintages and soothing rain.

Sweet Thing

It's four a.m.
She's rustling the verticals,
Jumping on me: WHAM!
Scratches my cuticle!

"Not now, baby"
She grrrs closer.
She kneads me, maybe.
An amateur poser,
She docs the "stare" thing
Before the alarm ring.

Day in and day out,
I deal with her
Rituals, rites, grrrr:
Her way to pray,
Manipulating my wants
with her instinctive rants.

I follow her orders,
Let her into twilight,
Rub my eye borders,
Hop back to dream flight.

Sea Foam

The power of ocean breezes

Waters the air like the mist on lilacs

And the dewy lips of youth.

It makes its way to stones

And canals and chipping tree bark.

The life force comes again,

Like angels calling out to the universe:

"Sea."

Waves of power, waves of white,

Crest and fall and break

Through night

Then trickling shells,

And sea foam.

Pleading

May I have a word with you,
silly heart?
Yes, you, sweet pea, pumpkin, ki ki.
kiss me in the corner and I'll blow my hair
onto your shoulder. Forget me not,
oh, lover.
Remember how my breath is sweet candy,
my tongue, spongy and wet,
sends messages along your flesh.
Weeks, months, years, perhaps,
melt into melancholy memories of love,
romance, timeless surrender and
sleepless nights.

Cosmo Girl Revisited

My hands are scarred from my children.
My womb was healed by their births.
My breasts worked; not made for augmentations.
My lips are thinning but I refuse to inject them with lies.
I should never have listened to your advice:
Your "How-to-please-a-Man" songs.
I refuse to starve myself for fake perfection.
I believed the "Dressing-for-successing"
And "Good-resumé-could-turn-into-cocktail-dress-after-5"
articles.
But every seven years I change.
Every seven years I am a new creature
With the same DNA and same scars,
a/k/a, my badges.
Au revoir. You don't need me anyway;
You have a new generation to deconstruct.

Coasting With Conscience

I frolic in the garden of gods and goddesses

With fairies and figments of the mind.

I frolic on roads with lotus flowers and chalices of rum,

On pastoral roads with warm breezes, lack of scrutiny and amoral love.

I stand naked in moonlight mist with arms outstretched

Defying smirking faces and complacent stares, knowing full well

It is my own judgment that matters.

I dance to a lyrical romanticism as my superego analyzed every step.

That sweet pantheism rebels the Victorian ethic

As it pushes the ideal into the lost dream where Arthur

Wandered and Prufrock lingered with Selwyn's

Yellow eyes, wasting away in early decay.

Birds are fed by the earth, free of karma.

With clenched fists, I open fingers and fall asleep

Back in the forest, after the gods have turned to stone,

And history has explained itself as fallen angels

Or ambitious egoists.

I reckon the desire to kiss the abyss

Without falling into black waters, drunk on a temptation

Or an ease that might be heaven or a nu age

Or nothing new at all. And in that reckoning

Comes the answer, the snap-snap of sacred eyes.

Your Majesty

Humbly, I bow to you, higher than a skyscraper,
For you are above me in all possible ways.
How so? Listen here; you are silk and I, paper.
You are intelligence while I'm a dumb stump.
You shine and radiate the Midas touch in rays
Of unearthly power, while I sit on the ledge, bump
Along life counting street cracks and feline strays.
You would never eat leftovers or sing my ditties.
You would never reach into your pocket for a tip.
You would never forecast your morning's drudgery
Nor cascade your worries into your daily itineraries.
You would rather die of thirst than ask for a sip
Of my drink or stop for milk at the pharmacy.
Humbly, I stretch out my hand to yours, a vapor
Of Eternity permeates…a scent you've worn for days
On end. Now, you fumble in your tapered
Skirt, the slit just high enough to hide a flabby rump,
And tight enough to conceal decades of blemishes.

The Urchins

They knew their stuff and clutched the soft spots

Of the ocean floor for that was their job, they were blind.

But in the weirdest sense, they saw the solitary sea floor:

the larger fish stealing food through murky fog-water, swimming faster,

pushing with mouths wide open. The shark-like fish

swallowed hard, desultory, robot-like.

Far away from the seashore, the urchins saw much more:

a small teakwood sewing machine with

ornate legs, apparently Dutch-made, lying in a Harlem Street

as November-slanted rain fast-warped the soft wood

and rusted the bobbins and motor.

The urchins closed their eyes.

It didn't matter that Frank, a homeless man, was slinking

along again in a valley of tears, desolate and drunk.

Looking into a puddle by the sewer

he saw his sad reflection, wiped his hand and stuck it into his pocket.

The urchins felt his presence though they were invisible to him.

There, the locket rubbed against his thumb.

So he took it out, cried as he saw the face of an angel

looking back at him. “It’ll be okay,” it seemed to whisper,

as he closed the clasp and let out sobs from the back

of his throat, in a man way, until he was able to choke them down.

Again at puddle, he saw a trapped pigeon stuck in the sewer slots.

With a quick maneuver, he pulled its broken wing out of the grate and it

Hobbled away

And the urchins rejoiced.

Ave Maria

He walked up to the altar wearing a black vest
over an ironed white shirt and black tie.
In his right hand, draped through his fingers,
was a black rosary. He touched his thick gray hair
with white strands and began to sing.
"Ave Maria," the familiar words were mused
in Italian and his voice seemed to project
white light with every word.
The patrons of the church stared in awe
as crystal tears blurred their vision.
His voice reverberated through the church,
and spiraled through the white rays shining
through the stained glass windows.
And in a final crescendo, he silently
walked off the altar into a shadowed
corner and began to move his lips in silent prayer
as his body remained an oracle of light.

The Dream

It was a fairy tale dream.
The kind with mythological icons and assertions
That tap into your memory and remind you,
Even in slumber, that you know the connection.
The “aha” moment comes deep in sleep
And your body twitches as you turn to the side.
Your pillow hears the murmurings, the isotopic
Half-screams that run the images in your mind’s eye.
It’s a Wells Fargo kind of deposit:
All thoughts are stacked and unchained
But there’s a dubious feeling, an unholy
Sense of disparity, a wasteland of disaster
That lurks there waiting
For your consciousness to catch up
To the discretion. Then, it’s over:
The nightmarish frenzy, the supposed understanding
Of absolutely nothing.

Rising From Ashes

I have dissipated into air.
I smile at sun and shine on dewy blossoms.
I look into horizons of anguish
And false smiles of survival
And relish spring breezes, the scent of voodoo rose.
It's been a long rendezvous in verdant pastures
Of blissful banishment and enchanting streams
Of weeping willows' song.
Ah, swaying again in droplets of vapor
Remembering the muse's words:
"Sweet Angel, revel in the words,
Wander and sow your seeds of ecstasy."
Had I forgotten?
Had I hardened into gross mass?
Had I frozen into an austere demeanor
Producing slavish insolence?
The seasons, that's it.
The seasons.
Yes, I remember the movement of stars,
And tides and moon's chanting of rhythms
And vibrations. How Glorious!
How sublime!

Sonnet 20

When you began to hate me it was a shock
Since all along we had been best of friends.
It happened slower than a mushroom sends
Its roots into the bark of a tree, amuck
And fallen to distress. Ours was a rock
Of love and trust and all good things; then trends
Like sex, fun, and texting notes put the bends
On our once smooth respect. It was a sock
To my self-esteem, a blow to my ego,
For you were no longer my confidante
And my sweet daughter bringing so much joy.
Will you always be my nemesis and foe?
Will I have to bribe you for what I want
Or will you come around, be my ally?

Love

Birds' songs permeate the air,

Rich with lilac and forsythia blossoms.

The sky is thick with mist and pollen.

GiGi

Lathering at the sides of your mouth,

Your tongue curled at the tip, you smile and let out a half bark.

Black and white collie and shepherd,

You were a soft mass of long fur.

Always excited to see us, you'd run up,

Cry out in dog laughter: "Hello. Glad you're home."
You'd jump on me, loving me, breathing, lapping my face.

Those darn claws had to be clipped, but mom was afraid to do it. Your big body could not grip the stairs.

Your appetite was enormous: and you begged for leftovers.

"I love you. I love you. I love you."

Your tears welled with saliva at the foot of the stair

When we'd leave you down in the basement.

Otherwise, you'd have torn right through the plastic covers

On the living room furniture. How long did you bark,

Waiting for our return, trying to get up the stairs,

The door locked,

Your hind legs giving in from arthritis?

You'd hear the key turn and smell us. "I'm down here!

Come and get me, please! I love you. I love you. I love you."

Thank You

You turned a nightmare into a joyous event.

It was magical how my tears turned to smiles.

Thank you.

How Do I Love You?

Soft as when I nestle my body in alignment with yours.
Quiet as when I listen to your breath and let mine catch the rhythm.
Passive as when I allow your thoughts to supersede mine.
Passionate as when we dance in the cool night air.
Laughing as when we relive past moments.
Soothing as when we massage each other's pain and kiss away the fears.
Serious as when the need for confrontation is inevitable.
Respectful as when we understand each other's truths and culture.
Playful as when we become teenagers again.
Comfortable as when we know exactly how to prepare morning coffee.
Peaceful as when we are one person.

Previously Published

"At the Montauk Club," *Brooklyn Poetry Circle*, 1989

"For Flora and Giovanni: Leaving the Nursing Home," *Walt's Corner*, 2018

"The Urchins," *Performance Poets Association Literary Review #22*, 2018

"Sonnet 20," *Towards Forgiveness*, 2010

"How Do I Love You," *Amore Love Poems*, 2016

About the Author

Denise Kolanovic is an English/ENL teacher and a poet. She has an MA in English from Brooklyn College and an MS in TESOL from Touro College; she has taught English for 15 years and ENL for 11 years. She first studied poetry with Collette Inez at The New School and later joined the Brooklyn Poetry Circle, New York Poetry Forum, Shelley Society, and National League of American Pen Women, of which she is past president of the All Cities Branch. Through All Cities Branch, she organized teen poetry contests and ran poetry workshops and scholarships for ESL students. She is active in Poets In Nassau, Performance Poets Association, and Bards Initiative and has been published nationally in several anthologies and journals including *Whispers and Shouts, Reckless Writing, Long Island Quarterly, Walt's Corner, Celiyd, Bards Annual, PPA Literary Review, Towards Forgiveness* and others. She won the Grabanier Sonnet award from Brooklyn College and the John Donne Award from Poetry Society of America. She co-edited three volumes of *Eve's Legacy*, a poetry anthology, and formed a poetry guild, "The Poet's Circle." She is the author of *Asphalt Sounds,* Fore Angels Press: 2004.

www.ingramcontent.com/pod-product-compliance
Ingram Content Group UK Ltd.
Pitfield, Milton Keynes, MK11 3LW, UK
UKHW020137250726
13967UKWH00002B/716

9 781716 455407